Making Boots, Sh

Marie Hartley and Joan Ingilby

Smith
Settle

First published in 1997 by
Smith Settle Ltd
Ilkley Road
Otley
West Yorkshire
LS21 3JP

© Marie Hartley and Joan Ingilby 1997

All rights reserved. No part of this book may be reproduced, stored or introduced into
a retrieval system, or transmitted in any form or by any means (electronic, mechanical,
photocopying, recording or otherwise) without the prior permission of Smith Settle Ltd.

The right of Marie Hartley and Joan Ingilby to be identified as the authors of this work has
been asserted by them in accordance with the Copyright, Designs and Patents Act 1988.

ISBN 1 85825 082 X

British Library Cataloguing-in-Publication data:
A catalogue record for this book is available from the British Library.

Set in Monotype Plantin

Designed, printed and bound by
SMITH SETTLE
Ilkley Road, Otley, West Yorkshire LS21 3JP

Introduction

Before the introduction of machinery to make footwear, individual boot, shoe and clog makers supplied the wants of their neighbourhoods. Their goods were hand-made and hand-sewn. In villages and towns they were by far the most numerous of craftsmen. For instance, in 1823 Richmond had twenty-six shoemakers; Reeth had eight, plus two clog and patten makers; Skipton had fourteen; and Hawes four and two clogmakers. They often combined two or more jobs. There was a clogger, boot, shoe and last maker at Richmond, and an auctioneer and clogger at Leyburn. In 1871 at a small village such as Keld in upper Swaledale there were Michael Wiseman, shoemaker, and Richard Parrington, inn-keeper, shoemaker, and small farmer at the Cathole Inn, and his son James, aged thirteen, apprentice. We ourselves remember Parrington, repairer, at Bridgend west of Keld in the 1930s.

Formerly they were called cordwainers, from Cordona in Spain, famous for its leather. Apprenticeships were usual. In 1826 John Cowling of Richmond served seven years as apprentice to his father, a shoemaker, to the trade of cordwainer. Besides these, itinerants, making and repairing footwear, went their rounds, and skilled journeymen toured the countryside. The latter were welcomed for help in busy times, and occasionally they brought new ideas. Many of these old shoemakers were characters, some given to drink we are told. Sitting in their work-shops day after day, they gossiped with callers, and set the world to rights.

As new machinery led to the mass production of footwear, the numbers of shoemakers gradually diminished over the last seventy or eighty years, and many had to seek new work or leave their native places. Most became repairers rather than makers, and now there are only occasional survivors.

However, in the mid-1960s we were able to interview and take photographs of two bespoke shoemakers making hand-sewn shoes: Arthur Inman of Grassington, then aged eighty-nine, who was born at Thorpe near Burnsall of a family of shoemakers, served an apprenticeship in Skipton, and moved to Grassington in 1929; and Frank Ward of Leyburn, who was apprenticed to his father, farmer and shoemaker, who employed two men. Our third and fourth were boot-makers: Tommy Hunter of Redmire aged eighty-six; and Chris Binks of Carlton in Coverdale, who made strong and market boots. These two had made their last hand-sewn pairs in the 1940s, but were still working as repairers.

We also met the Haws of Thoralby in Bishopdale, who had once four men working for them, and who had rounds on each day of the week, going as far as Kettlewell in Wharfedale. They all spoke of the long hours of work, working up to eight or nine o'clock at night by the light of oil lamps; of the journeys into other dales to sell their wares, carrying heavy boots, or travelling by horse and cart; of payment every six months or yearly, as was the custom; and of strong boots selling for 18s a pair.

The shoemaker's workshop contained a shoe-maker's bench — a long, low stool with a seat at one end and a tray for materials at the other. Depending on the craftsman being left- or right-handed, the tray was on the left or right. They were of necessity ambidextrous, and they always wore a hand leather. There was a measuring stick, a board on which to cut leather, a clicking knife, a stirrup (leather belt), a lapstone, lasting pincers, hammers, several awls, a sewing machine, hemp thread, a rack for lasts, a container for water, a bench for callers, rolls or bends of leather, a pan for boiling up the resin, pitch and tallow or beeswax for waxing the sewing thread, and a stove for warmth.

In the last century, many towns had tanyards for sources of leather, and the great Lammas Leather Fair at Settle drew shoemakers and saddlers from far and wide. But in this century, dealers came round selling the different leathers suited to the parts of a shoe and the work in hand. When buying leather the shoemaker often begged an apron of sheepskin, the cheapest.

A boot or shoe was made up of insole, uppers, welt, sole and heel, with toe puffs and heel stiffeners to fit in. The maker first drew round the customer's foot on paper on the floor, and took measurements. The uppers were cut out from patterns, and sewn together on the sewing machine, called closing. The insole was prepared, and placed on a last chosen to conform with the customer's foot. Heel stiffeners and toe puffs were inserted. The uppers were pulled over the last with the lasting pincers, called lasting. Then the upper components, welt and insole were stitched together with one seam using both ends of the thread. At the toe, six thicknesses of leather had to be sewn through — insole, lining, toe puff, extra layer for toe, welt and upper. The sole is then fitted on and stitched to the welt. Heels had to be nailed on in lifts.

Taking out the last was the final job. It took twenty-eight hours to make a pair of shoes, and four pairs of boots made in a week was good work.

Apprentices started off by repairing shoes or preparing the sewing thread, called casting. Hemp was employed, using four to ten cords (strands) according to the work. The length of thread was eleven feet, judged by two and a half times the outstretched arms. It was looped over a nail, twisted and rubbed on the side of the leg, then waxed with a mixture of resin, pitch and oil, boiled together in a pan. Formerly to make a wax end for sewing, expensive wild boar bristles from the Black Forest were used, but nylon has replaced these. Twisting on wax ends was an art in in itself. (Thread is now bought ready prepared.)

Clogs, with leather uppers and wooden soles, differ from boots in that they are mostly nailed, not sewn together. They were associated with footwear for farmers, millworkers, quarrymen and foundry workers, or anyone employed in wet conditions. Their merit was that they were cheap, and kept the feet dry. Formerly in the West Riding clogmakers flourished, and firms such as Waltons at Halifax and Walkleys at Hebden Bridge produced them in quantity. Walkleys specialised in clog soles. Other firms made the metal clasps, toe bands and so on, or supplied clog irons to be nailed on the wooden soles. All these except Walkleys have gone, but this firm still supplies wooden soles, and also sells 15-20,000 pairs of clogs a year.

Formerly the clogger fashioned his own soles from a split log, and to do so used three stock knives (see pages 32-4). The upper was cut out of cow hide from patterns, sewn together and then nailed to the sole, and toe bands and clasps fixed — a job taking three to four hours. Whereas mass-produced goods finished off hand-sewn boots and shoes, Wellington boots and other influences brought about the decline of the clog.

However, the Nelsons at Settle — Jim and his son Daniel — are as far as we know the last practising boot, shoe and clog-makers in the Dales. Daniel is the fifth generation of shoemakers who have been at Settle since 1847. In 1996 we took photographs of him making a clog in red and green leather. Such is their trade in men's heavy clogs, elegant ladies' and small children's that they can hardly keep up with the demand. We thank them for their help.

Photographic Acknowledgements

We wish to thank Mr J A Rawcliffe for the photograph on page 8; Mrs D Tattersall for that on page 2; and Mr J E Utley for page 33.

Old-time shoemaker Alf Allinson, at Horton-in-Ribblesdale in the 1930s.

John Bentham, itinerant shoemaker, who lived at Horton-in-Ribblesdale. He is using an awl with the boot held firm by a stirrup. (1880s.)

Arthur Inman 'casting' — making thread for stitching by measuring eight hemp cords (strands) about eleven feet, followed by twisting and waxing.

Having measured the foot and selected a last, he prepares the insole for stitching by piercing holes in and out with the sewing awl. The insole is then tacked to the last.

Pulling the upper on to the last with lasting pincers, known as 'lasting'.

Sewing the upper components, welt and insole together with one seam
using both ends of the thread.

The sole, having been soaked in water, is moulded to the insole,
ready for sewing to the welt. He is using a stirrup.

Paring the sole whilst wet to the correct shape.

Sewing on the sole, beginning at the heel.

Frank Ward twisting on a new wax end on to the thread. This was an art in itself. Nylon is used instead of the former wild boar's bristle.

Using the sewing awl.

Piercing the welt, holding close to the upper with the left thumb and forefinger whilst the awl is passed through.

Sewing the welt, pulling either way. Sewing was hard work,
but Frank Ward told us that he loved it.

Trimming round.

Tommy Hunter cutting leather on a cutting board — carefully so as not to waste leather. The board had to be smooth, and was planed from time to time by a joiner.

At the sewing machine used for stitching the parts of the upper (known as 'closing').

Braying the sole after soaking in water on a lapstone to tighten the grain.

Trimming off the finished boot.

Putting nails into a boot sole. Note the rack for lasts,
and below a bench for customers and friends.

Chris Binks removing
a sole for repairs.

Using lasting pincers.

Using an awl.

Choosing lasts.

CLOGS

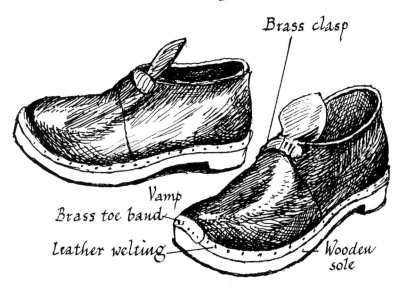

Brass clasp

Vamp

Brass toe band

Leather welting

Wooden sole

Clasp Clogs

Shaping clog soles from rough blocks of wood with a
stock knife, at Walkleys Clogs of Hebden Bridge. The
knife is hooked on a ring on the horse. Alder, beech,
birch and sycamore were used for soles.

There were three types of stock knife — the first shown on
the page opposite. The second is the hollower *(pictured)*
which hollows out the sole, and the third the gripper
(on the next page) which cuts a channel on which
the uppers are nailed.

William Grainger of Hawes using the gripper to make a channel round the edge of the sole on which the upper is fitted. (c1950.)

Miles Bainbridge at Sedbergh lasting the upper using a light hammer. At the age of fifteen he was apprenticed to Yares of Kirkby Stephen during the 1914–1918 war. Working hard, he could make twelve pairs of clogs in a day.

J V Brown, clogger at Airton, Malhamdale, using a clogger's stiddy. He and his father supplied the people of Malhamdale with clogs for over seventy years.

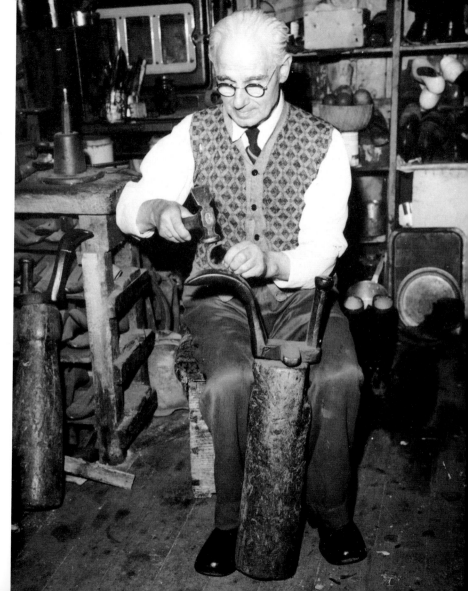

R Greenwood, clogger at Haworth, outside his shop, its windows filled with clogs.

Daniel Nelson at Settle starting to make a clog. He marks out the leather for uppers from patterns. He is making a pair, so has two lots of three pieces.

Cutting out the pieces with
a clicking knife.

Skiving, that is thinning the edges in order to make a neat seam when stitching.

Sewing the pieces together on a sewing machine (closing).
Next, insert the heel stiffener and stick.

He puts a last on the
sole and fits the
upper.

Pulling the upper onto the
sole with lasting pincers
('lasting').

He nails the upper on to the sole, and next puts on the toe band, a small sheet-iron plate to protect the toe of the sole.

Nailing the leather welting
all round to cover the join.

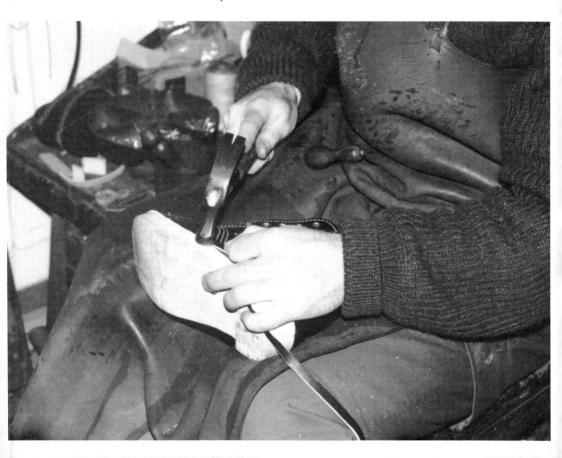

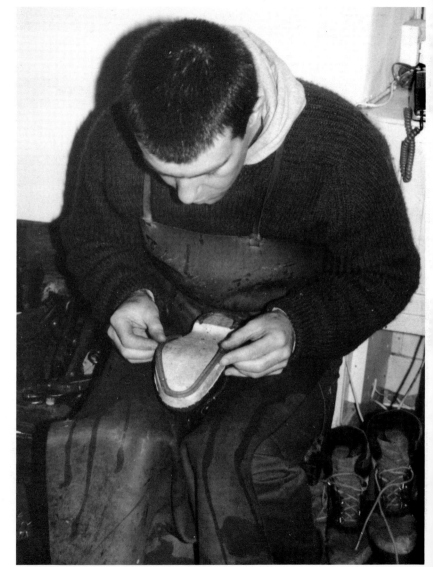

Finally he nails on clog irons on the sole and heel.